MAXIMUM
INTEGRITY

Leadership Insights from the Psalms

Stan Toler and Jerry Brecheisen

BEACON HILL PRESS
OF KANSAS CITY

ISBN-13: 978-0-8341-2283-3
ISBN-10: 0-8341-2283-9

Printed in the
United States of America

Cover Design: J.R. Caines
Interior Design: Sharon Page

Library of Congress Cataloging-in-Publication Data

Toler, Stan.
  Maximum integrity : leadership insights from the Psalms / Stan Toler and Jerry Brecheisen.
    p. cm.
  Includes bibliographical references (p.   ).
  ISBN-13: 978-0-8341-2283-3 (pbk.)
  ISBN-10: 0-8341-2283-9 (pbk.)
  1. Bible. O.T. Psalms—Criticism, interpretation, etc. 2. Leadership. I. Brecheisen, Jerry. II. Title.
  BS1430.6.L4T65   2006
  223'.206—dc22

2006029544

10 9 8 7 6 5 4 3 2 1

CONTENTS

CONTENTS

INTRODUCTION

Great leaders are great followers. Yet they are selective about whom they will follow. They want someone who has survived the tough times and who has raised his or her followers to greater heights. They are not looking for someone who is perfect but one who—through good times and bad—worked diligently to be a servant of God and a servant-leader to those he or she has led.

ADVICE FROM A GREAT LEADER

David, the great king of Israel and major writer of the Psalms, was such a leader. God promoted him up the corporate ladder of His kingdom, from shepherding sheep to finally shepherding God's own people as their king. Along the way, David devised battle plans that defeated Israel's fiercest foes. He excelled in human resources, successfully contending with the jealous infighting of his kingdom—and even that of his own family. And he faced his toughest battle when dealing with personal issues that included lust and greed, failure and recovery, guilt and forgiveness. His leadership model is one that you can follow. In one way or another, he has gone through just about everything you will face in modern leadership.

WINDOW TO A LEADER'S SOUL

You can read about David the king in the history books of the Old Testament (1 Samuel, 2 Samuel, 1 Chronicles, 2 Chronicles). But to get into the heart of David the man, to find out what really made him tick, you'll need to read his own words. He was not only a gifted leader but also a gifted writer of songs and poems, all of which were open windows to his soul, tracking the path of his leadership.

These writings are included in the book of the Bible we know as the Psalms. They are a beautiful combination of mountaintop and valley experiences that people have turned to for ages. Whether David is singing the blues or voicing an oratorio of praise, he is opening his heart to show you how to be victorious when facing your own leadership challenges. David holds nothing back—he lays bare his emotions across the pages of the best-selling book of all time—the Bible.

LEADERS HAVE LOOKED TO THEM

Great leaders have leaned upon the Psalms for help, comfort, and guidance. Jonah's prayer in the belly of a big fish was dotted with the words of the Psalms. Jesus quoted them as He walked dusty roads or sat teaching in the Temple. He sang them in harmonic a cappella with His disciples around the supper table at their last meeting. And then He uttered their prophecies in His last words on the Cross.

The Early Church warmed itself with the invigorating glow

of the Psalms as it faced the cold winds of opposition. The apostles used them as the foundation for their public sermons and private letters. Peter used their truths to explain the doctrines of God on the Day of Pentecost. Paul, the missionary and theological giant, not only taught from them but also surely wrapped his heart in them as he experienced the dungeons and dangers of his volatile leadership ministry.

MANUAL FOR EFFECTIVE LEADERSHIP

The Psalms reflect our own lives as well. Eugene Peterson said, "People look into the mirror to see how they look; they look into the Psalms to find out who they are." John Calvin referred to them as "an anatomy of all parts of the soul." John Wesley said they were "a rich treasury of devotion, which the wisdom of God has provided to supply the wants of his children in all generations!"

We bring you several highly revered psalms, almost all by David. They will entice you to follow his great example of leadership—his actions and reactions—when the corporate tigers add you to their lunch menu. They will also provide a miniseminar on effective leadership and personal growth, whether the sun is shining or the clouds are gathering. Read them aloud or read them silently. When you're having a day when everything (and everyone) seems to be working in sync, read the rejoicing psalms. Then on those inevitable days when you're faced with corporate or personal crisis, read the reflective songs.

But read them with a sense of ultimate victory. Discover

that even when David the king was abandoned by both friend and foe, God stood with him. These psalms are for your personal triumphs or tragedies. We have included our own reflections with these great writings—reflections born from those times when we paused and entered the sanctuary of the Psalms during our own life journey. We will use just a few verses of each psalm to present several larger-than-life principles. But of course, we encourage you to read each psalm in its entirety.

Whether you are a shepherd, king, or someone in between, we trust that you will find help for your soul and reinforcement for your personal mission.

—Stan Toler and Jerry Brecheisen

PSALM 1

¹Blessed is the man
 who does not walk in the counsel of the wicked
 or stand in the way of sinners
 or sit in the seat of mockers.
²But his delight is in the law of the LORD,
 and on his law he meditates day and night.
³He is like a tree planted by streams of water,
 which yields its fruit in season
 and whose leaf does not wither.
 Whatever he does prospers.

ONE
FORMULA FOR SUCCESS

As leaders, we are success-driven. Whether we're seeking the advancement of our company and its products and services or seeking the success of those who work for and with us, we thrive on a positive bottom line.

How would you like to be successful in everything you do? How would you like to get up in the morning and know that no matter what you do, you will succeed? Your confidence level would soar like an eagle!

UNLIMITED HAPPINESS AND JOY

On top of an incredible success rate, how would you like to experience unlimited happiness and joy? Good days that would far outweigh your bad days? Enough strength for every task? How would you like to be truly blessed?

Do we have your attention yet?

You may be asking, "What is the formula?" Granted, there is no substitute for prayerful planning, hard work, and effective management. But there are biblical principles that can add spiritual fuel to the fires of your vision and effort.

Psalm 1 categorizes some basic rules of the road for your personal and corporate journey—rules that not only help make you a true success but also add personal joy. They consist of *avoiding three things* and *adding one important thing* on a daily basis.

The three things you must avoid are these:

1. Walking in the counsel of the wicked
2. Standing in the way of sinners
3. Sitting in the seat of mockers

GOOD ADVICE

Do you see the landmines those cautions are uncovering? Let's consider them. First, there is a caution against listening to "the counsel of the wicked." So what's wrong with gathering input from various sources? Isn't it wise to get counsel from several people before making a decision? Yes—to a degree. But let's face it. Not all advice is good advice. You learned that the first time you asked for directions and heard the words "You can't miss it."

The writer of Proverbs says, "There is a way that seems right to a man, but in the end it leads to death" (14:12). Author G. K. Chesterton once said, "I owe my success to having listened respectfully to the very best advice, and then going away and doing the exact opposite." He wasn't saying that all advice is wrong. He was saying that advice coming from the *right source* is more valuable to him.

In the days before MRIs and virtual patients, nurses and doctors in training primarily used stethoscopes to listen to lungs in order to detect problems. How did they learn to hear the difference between healthy lungs and unhealthy lungs? They listened to the sounds of healthy lungs—lungs that were strong and clear. Then when they were with real patients and heard anything that didn't sound like healthy lungs, they knew there was a problem.

In the same way, usually the best advice comes from those who are spiritually healthy, who inhale and exhale the truth of God's Word—those who have a vital relationship with God through faith in the Lord Jesus Christ. The Bible says, "The natural man doesn't understand spiritual truths" (1 Cor. 2:14, author's paraphrase). True success, then, comes from listening to persons who do understand such truths, who are led by the Spirit of God rather than just human instinct or experience. Psalm 37:30 states, "The godly offer good counsel; they know what is right from wrong" (NLT).

If you focus on hearing from those who obey God, follow God, and love God and you then hear something else, you'll know it is unhealthy and you can choose to ignore it. Those who want true success will reject "the counsel of the wicked."

The Wicked

Who are "the wicked"? Do they look like monsters? Are people afraid of them as they pass in the street? Not necessarily. They look like everyone else. Some are tall, some are short, some are handsome or pretty, and some are uglier than a rotting fencepost. Probably if you would look at them closely, you couldn't even spot their wickedness. Why? Because it's on the inside. The wicked have a hidden agenda that doesn't include God's advice.

It's a problem that goes all the way back to the beginning of time. Genesis, the first book of the Bible, describes them: "The LORD saw how great man's wickedness on the earth had become, and that every inclination of the thoughts of his heart was only evil all the time" (Gen. 6:5). Likewise the wicked constantly seek their own pleasure rather than the goodness of God.

Oh, they may *look good* or even *do good things,* but their goodness is self-perpetuated. Their own counsel is their guide. They are inclined to do their thing rather than God's will. Consequently, they move farther away from God. If you want to walk in God's way, you'll choose His advice over the advice of the wicked.

The Sinner

The second caution is, Don't "stand in the way of sinners." It suggests not copying the life or lifestyle of others—especially if they are not people of faith. We are all imitators. As leaders, we follow the examples of those we admire.

You pick up ideas from many. You are constantly looking to others for effective ways to perform your duties. But if you are to have true success in life—personally or corporately—you'll avoid following the example of sinners, following those who ignore God. David practiced the principle: "I have followed your commands, which have kept me from going along with cruel and evil people" (Ps. 17:4, NLT).

Just who is a sinner? A sinner, by definition, is someone who disobeys God's law on purpose—who knows what is right and chooses what is wrong instead (see James 4:17). We speak of sinners as those who are lost. (As the great hymn "Amazing Grace" says, "I once was lost, but now am found.") Why follow someone who is lost? It's the old story of a passenger asking the driver if she knows where she's going. The driver says, "No, but we're making good time!"

Driving on the *fast track* doesn't mean that a person is necessarily *on track*. Faith-based success adapts to meet society's demands, but it doesn't adopt its lifestyles.

The Mockers

Finally, we are told not to join with those who "sit in the seat of mockers." There are many who seem to have it together like a computer network at Microsoft, yet they lack an inner desire for God. Their spiritual neglect mocks God. They are self-sufficient, not God-sufficient. They do not pray or search the Scriptures to seek His will; they do not acknowledge Him as their Father.

We are not to treat mockers as spiritual lepers, but in essence, we're told not to join their country club. If you want to be blessed (spiritually happy), you will avoid going into partnership with the godless. The Bible warns not to be joined with unbelievers (2 Cor. 6:14). It's like putting a deer and a tiger on the same doubles team for a tennis match!

THE BOOK

You've seen three things to *avoid*. But what is the one thing you are to *do* in order to have personal or corporate success and happiness?

According to this psalm, you must regularly turn to the principles of the Bible. Even before you talk to your associates, you should hear from God. Daily Bible reading is a means to spiritual success: "Study this Book of the Law continually. Meditate on it day and night so you may be sure to obey all that is written in it. Only then will you succeed" (Josh. 1:8, NLT).

That most wonderful and best-selling book of all time is the story of God's interaction with His people. It lists spiritual laws and principles that, if obeyed, will result in inner joy—even when outward circumstances are discouraging.

The Bible has been described as a love letter from God. It's full of God's affirmation for those who have placed their trust in Him. And its pages are equally filled with life-giving resources that lead to a full, abundant life (see John 10:10).

Our foreparents, Adam and Eve, were offered eternal life from one tree in the Garden of Eden. Instead they chose the tree of knowledge and tried to be godlike in their wisdom. It resulted in banishment from paradise and death at the end of a hard life.

You don't have to eat in some spiritual fast-food restaurant. You're invited to a sit-down dinner in God's five-star restaurant. Psalm 119:103 says, "How sweet are your words to my taste, sweeter than honey to my mouth!"

SECOND CHANCE

The Bible is also a book of second chances. It is like a global positioning satellite, pointing us back to God when we've strayed off course. Second Timothy 3:15 says that the Bible is able to make you wise for salvation through faith in Christ Jesus. Psalm 1 is a psalm of forgiveness, earthly understanding, and eternal and abundant life.

So, if you're facing life-changing decisions—decisions that will result in success or failure, happiness or sorrow, rest in God's advice. Take a *right turn* to the Word of God. You'll discover that it has been written with you in mind.

Follow its road clearly. You may not experience the good life financially, but you'll surely experience a great life spiritually! David likens that choice to becoming "a tree planted by streams of water, which yields its fruit in season." It is a refreshing life that results in purpose and production: "whatever he does prospers."

What a life!

PSALM 2

[10]Therefore, you kings, be wise;
    be warned, you rulers of the earth.
[11]Serve the LORD with fear
    and rejoice with trembling.
[12]Kiss the Son, lest he be angry
    and you be destroyed in your way,
    for his wrath can flare up in a moment.
    Blessed are all who take refuge in him.

TWO
FIGHTING FEAR WITH FEAR

Being a leader is often exciting and rewarding, like leading a marching band in a Christmas parade. But you know that there are days when you would rather run and hide, when it seems as if you're leading a parade through a summer storm and the band is marching in the four directions at once! Events transpire (or conspire) that cause you to fear—fear for your projects, your career, or even your sanity.

President Franklin D. Roosevelt once said, "We have nothing to fear but fear itself." But that may not always be the case. There is value in fear. Fear is a natural—and good—characteristic. Without fear, you wouldn't survive. Fear keeps you from walking into oncoming traffic or playing with fire. Fear keeps you from reaching into the lion's cage at the zoo. Fear is self-preserving. It causes you to fight—to protect yourself in times of danger.

There are rational fears that protect you, and there are irrational fears that can rob you of the joy of life—and true success. In psychology irrational fears are known as phobias. Scholars have identified more than 500 phobias, such as alektorophobia (the fear of chickens), pentheraphobia (the fear of your mother-in-law), or arachibutyrophobia (the fear of peanut butter sticking to the roof of your mouth).

HEALTHY AND UNHEALTHY FEAR

Essentially, fear can be healthy! For example, the fear of making the wrong decision may slow you down long enough to reflect: *Do I have my spiritual, financial, and physical ducks in a row before I commit myself to this course of action?* As long as fear doesn't cause *analysis paralysis*—keeping you from necessary action—it can be healthy and reasonable.

Fear becomes unhealthy and unreasonable when it keeps you from making any decision at all! Fear is especially unhealthy when it focuses on others. One of the greatest leadership roadblocks is the fear of others—knowing what you should do but not doing it because of what others may think.

This is where you will fight fear with fear!

FEAR THE LORD

Read the verses from Ps. 2. In verses 10 and 11, we read that kings (leaders) become wise (spiritually perceptive) by serving the Lord with fear. *Doesn't that put the entire "God is great and God is good" childhood prayer on the shelf?* No. Sometimes we are to spiritually tremble with fear before God.

To fear God means far more than showing respect for God. The Hebrew word used for fear in this verse *doesn't* mean "to respect." David chose a word that means "to be afraid," to be shake-in-your-boots afraid. It comes from the belief that God is the CEO of life; He is absolutely in control of every molecule or minute. And He ultimately decides your future. His word is

THREE

NO MORE MINIMUM INTEGRITY

Early into the third millennium, the collapse of business giants Enron and WorldCom shocked the corporate world. The fallout brought a new focus on business ethics and personal integrity. But as you see in Ps. 15, the subject of integrity has always been a hot topic. It was on the mind of King David thousands of years before these epic failures. Integrity is the key to being the leader God wants you to be.

There is no such thing as minimum integrity in God's eyes. If you are looking for ethical shortcuts, you won't find them in Scripture. The Bible has a standard for integrity—seen in the lives of very human people, in very human situations.

The psalmist's question: "Who may dwell in your sanctuary?" The answer: "He whose walk is blameless." People with maximum integrity, who haven't bartered their values in the marketplace, are sanctuary dwellers. They walk in the favor of God and dwell in the sanctuary of His presence.

EXAMPLES IN THE BIBLE

In Bible times, people of faith personalized integrity. The Old Testament leader Joseph is a case in point. Sold as a slave by his brothers, he performed duties forced upon him in captivity with excellence and enthusiasm, and soon rose to a level of prominence with his owner, Potiphar. As a result of Joseph's personal integrity and God-given wisdom, he was placed in charge of Potiphar's entire household. Perhaps the apostle Paul was thinking of him when he wrote to the Colossians, "Slaves, obey your masters in all things. Do not obey just when they are watching you, to gain their favor, but serve them honestly, because you respect the Lord. In all the work you are doing, work the best you can. Work as if you were doing it for the Lord, not for people" (Col. 3:22-23, NCV).

We assume that none of you reading this book is actually a slave (though some of you may feel like it at times). Yet substitute the word *employee* for *slave* and *employer* for *master* and the context is the same. You are not given the option of obeying only those whom you like. In modern terms Paul is saying, "Don't just do what you are supposed to do when your boss is watching; be faithful at all times, knowing that your ultimate supervisor is God."

J. C. Watts said, "Character is doing the right thing when nobody's looking."[1] But everybody *is* looking. Living a life of integrity is not easy. As a matter of fact, it is impossible to do on your own. Joseph knew that left to himself, he would fail. But there was a God factor in his life and leadership. The Lord was with him—as He will be with you today.

Look at Ps. 15 again. God's favor rests on those with integrity in four areas.

Spiritual

The first (and most important) area is spiritual integrity: "He . . . who speaks the truth from his heart" (v. 2). A leader with spiritual integrity practices truth. People who have spiritual integrity delight in telling the truth. They live their life as if it were displayed on a giant screen that could be seen by everyone.

And what is the source of that truth-living? God's Word says, "A good person produces good words from a good heart, and an evil person produces evil words from an evil heart" (Matt. 12:35, NLT). A heart filled with God's truth overflows with truthful words. The result is openness and honesty—being truthful about yourself and others and keeping your word, even when it isn't convenient.

Let's be frank. Honesty is always the best policy, but it doesn't always lead to an election or a promotion! However, it does lead to something even better. It leads to spiritual stability—which in turn leads to overall success. Psalm 15:5 reveals the bottom line: "He who does these things will never be shaken."

Social

The second area deals with your relationship to family, friends, or associates—social integrity. Jesus implied that our lives are both vertical and horizontal—that our relationship with God is reflected in our relationship with others. In response to a question about the greatest commandment, Jesus said, "'Love the Lord your God with all your heart, all your soul, and all your mind.' This is the first and greatest commandment. A second is equally important: 'Love your neighbor as yourself.' All the other commandments and all the demands of the prophets are based on these two commandments" (Matt. 22:37-40, NLT).

David spoke of that kind of integrity in Ps. 15. The one who dwells in God's sanctuary—in God's favor—"has no slander on his tongue" (v. 3). That person doesn't build himself or herself up by putting others down! In a leader's life, it simply means that true success isn't achieved on the backs of others. You know that negative words can do irreparable harm to someone's personal or vocational reputation. If you will be a leader with social integrity, you will speak truthfully, carefully, and purposefully.

Moral

In an age when Internet porn can be downloaded to a cell phone and road rage is as common as a road sign, the third area, moral integrity, is a prized characteristic. The leader who dwells in God's sanctuary—who lives in His favor—is one "who despises a vile man" (v. 4). *Wait a minute! You just said I should love my neighbor. How can we love someone and despise him or her at the same time?* Moral integrity doesn't necessarily separate you from a person who is immoral; it simply separates you from their immorality. In John 17:15-16, Jesus prays, "Just as I didn't join the world's ways. I'm not asking that you take them out of the world but that you guard them from the Evil One. They are no more defined by the world than I am defined by the world" (TM).

The call of the wild will always echo in your ears. But God is able to keep you from wandering. His discernment and His grace are sufficient: "No test or temptation that comes your way is beyond the course of what others have had to face. All you need to remember is that God will never let you down; he'll never let you be pushed past your limit; he'll always be there to help you come through it" (1 Cor. 10:13, TM).

Financial

The area of financial integrity has always been a factor in the fallen empires of the corporate world. Leaders who dwell in God's sanctuary—who lead in God's favor—have an open-book policy. Their finances are safe under scrutiny. And their financial dealings are graced with generosity. David described them as those "who [lend their] money without usury and [do] not accept a bribe against the innocent" (Ps. 15:5).

Religious leaders are especially vulnerable to the audits of the enemy. The world delights in the financial failures of the church. If you will find favor with God—and with humankind—you will make every effort to be responsible in the area of your finances. Financial integrity isn't optional. It is essential to the soul and important to the building of the Kingdom.

The Lord is with you today to help you walk with the highest integrity. Choose to be a Joseph—even in the land of the enemy.

PSALM 19

⁷The law of the LORD is perfect,
　　reviving the soul.
　　The statutes of the LORD are trustworthy,
　　making wise the simple.
⁸The precepts of the LORD are right,
　　giving joy to the heart.
　　The commands of the LORD are radiant,
　　giving light to the eyes.
⁹The fear of the LORD is pure,
　　enduring forever.
　　The ordinances of the LORD are sure
　　and altogether righteous.
¹⁰They are more precious than gold,
　　than much pure gold;
　　they are sweeter than honey,
　　than honey from the comb.
¹¹By them is your servant warned;
　　in keeping them there is great reward.

FOUR
READING THE INSTRUCTIONS

Reading is essential to every profession. Whether you read books, magazines, business reports, or scan the instructions for putting a new ink cartridge in the printer, what you read is what you reap. King David was a reader, and God was his favorite author: "The law of the LORD is perfect" (Ps. 19:7). Unlike us, he didn't have access to the "library" of the Bible (66 separate books within one book). He didn't have an online Bible. He didn't carry a handheld computer with the Scriptures downloaded. He read the laws of the Lord that were written on papyrus. To David, the effect of God's Word was worth the effort in reading God's Word.

MANUAL FOR LIVING

It's exciting! God loved you enough to give you a manual for living. That's more than you'll get when you buy a Swiss army knife! Reading the Bible is like reading the instructions. Consequently, it shouldn't be just scanned. It should be studied, if you will reap its benefits. The New Testament writer Paul said, "There's nothing like the written Word of God for showing you the way to salvation through faith in Christ Jesus. Every part of Scripture is God-breathed and useful one way or another—showing us truth, exposing our rebellion, correcting our mistakes, training us to live God's way. Through the Word we are put together and shaped up for the tasks God has for us" (2 Tim. 3:16-17, TM).

Freeing and Refreshing

Far from being a straightjacket or wet blanket, David found the laws of God's Word to be freeing and refreshing. The great writer Charles Dickens said of just one part of the Bible, "The New Testament is the very best book that ever was or will be known in the world."

Notice what David says in Ps. 19 about the benefits of reading the Scriptures. *First, David says God's Word revives the soul* (v. 7). If you are suffering the effects of borderline—or full-blown—leader burnout, God's instructions are just what you need. For example, you'll discover that God has an administrative plan that will help you relieve stress—and meet your goals. Moses discovered it during a visit from his father-in-law (Exod. 18).

One day Moses went to work—and took his father-in-law with him! It was to be a long day; Moses was a leader-judge over the questions and concerns of nearly a half-million people. His father-in-law didn't approve of his long hours or his leadership! He said, "What you are doing is not good. You and these people who come to you will only wear yourselves out. The work is too heavy for you; you cannot handle it alone" (vv. 17-18).

Moses was working from dawn to dusk, handling the problems of the people by himself. His father-in-law had a better plan —delegation.

You must be the people's representative before God and bring their disputes to him. Teach them the decrees and laws, and show them the way to live and the duties they are to perform. But select capable men from all the people—men who fear God, trustworthy men who hate dishonest gain—and appoint them as officials over thousands, hundreds, fifties and tens *(vv. 19-21)*.

God's Word is not only enlightening—it's reviving!

Joyful and Exciting

The second benefit of reading the Scriptures is for their emotional lift. David said they "give joy to the heart" and "light to the eyes" (Ps. 19:8). It doesn't take many days on any job to realize that the job description was more promising than the job! Leadership is tedious. Often the *same things* need to be said to the *same people.* Often you wonder if you are accomplishing anything. When the glow begins to dim, it's a good time to read encouraging words.

The Bible says, "If God is for us, who can be against us?" (Rom. 8:31). Read the Bible and you'll begin to understand that leadership is teamwork—and you're teamed with God himself.

Enduring and Holy

Another benefit of reading God's Word is holiness. David said, "The ordinances of the LORD are sure and altogether righteous" (Ps. 19:9). In another psalm, he says that reading those ordinances leads to holy living: "I have hidden your word in my heart, that I might not sin against you" (119:11, NLT). God's enduring Word is the source of wisdom in making right and holy choices.

Do you really need to add more reading to your day? The answer is an overwhelming yes! When Jesus said, "Man does not live on bread alone" (Matt. 4:4), He wasn't talking about adding nachos or cheesecake to your diet. The Scriptures (God's instructions) are in the food pyramid for your spiritual and vocational health.

Here are some tips for making Bible reading a part of a complete, healthy diet for your soul.

- Select a version of the Bible you feel comfortable with. There are many different versions with a variety of writing styles. You may like an older, tried-and-true version such as the King James Version or the *Revised Standard Version*. Or you may prefer one of the newer translations or paraphrases. For the most part, it really doesn't matter as long as you are reading the Bible!

- Set aside a specific time each day for Bible reading. This will help you make a habit out of reading God's Word.

- Keep a notebook and pen handy to jot down your thoughts and feelings as you read. This journal will be a record of your spiritual journey.

- Read prayerfully. If there is something you don't understand, ask God to show you what the passage means—especially as it relates to your life. If a passage is particularly sticky, you may also want to consult a good commentary. God wants you to understand what He has written to you.

• Don't be afraid to mark in your Bible. Underline verses that have special meaning to you. Write notes in your margins that help you understand certain passages. Think of your Bible as a working notebook, not a museum piece.

In one sense, leadership is *led-ship*. And those who follow the instructions have a better chance of getting it right!

PSALM 23 (NKJV)

[1]The LORD is my shepherd;
    I shall not want.
[2]He makes me to lie down in green pastures;
    He leads me beside the still waters.
[3]He restores my soul;
    He leads me in the paths of righteousness
    for His name's sake.
[4]Yea, though I walk through the valley of the shadow
of death,
    I will fear no evil;
    for You are with me;
    Your rod and Your staff, they comfort me.
[5]You prepare a table before me in the presence of
my enemies;
    You anoint my head with oil;
    my cup runs over.
[6]Surely goodness and mercy shall follow me
    all the days of my life;
    and I will dwell in the house of the LORD
    forever.

FIVE
SHEPHERD AND SHEEP

There was a man who needed an inexpensive place to live. After a long search through the classified ads, he accepted an offer to live on a small farm in exchange for taking care of a few sheep. *What's the big deal about taking care of a handful of sheep?* he thought. On the first day of his new job, he discovered the "big deal!"

Part of his job description was to keep the sheep inside the fences. He quickly discovered that sheep and fences are political opponents. Sheep like grazing privileges, anywhere their hunger leads them. If the grass looks greener on the other side (and it always does), they will find a way over, under, or through the fence to the greener grass.

Soon the reluctant shepherd was spending his days alternately chasing sheep, tackling sheep, dragging sheep back to the pen, or giving them PowerPoint presentations on sheep etiquette! The shepherd got a cheap room, all right, but he learned a costly lesson. Left to themselves, sheep will find a way to get into trouble. That's why they need shepherds.

People are a lot like sheep. They don't like fences. They're always eyeing greener pastures. They're usually on opposite sides of the argument. They usually find a way to get into trouble. And they desperately need a shepherd.

David the king was once David the shepherd. He knew sheep. And he knew people. In his beloved 23rd psalm he blends the insights of a shepherd and a king into an analogy that has comforted the lost or troubled for centuries.

Here is the good news: There is a Good Shepherd who loves caring for sheep. The bad news? We are the sheep. And we need a shepherd.

Pastors are often called shepherds. Does this mean that a pastor is smarter than those in the rest of the congregation? Of course not! Pastors simply fulfill their duty as earthly representatives of the Great Shepherd. Their responsibility is to provide for the sheep who call their church home. They feed them with the Word. They protect them from their enemy. They search for them when they wander. And they welcome them back home at Christmas and Easter.

A middle-aged pastor had just taken a new church in another state. Once he was settled in, he decided to join a local civic organization. The organization's president was happy to greet the minister, but she told the minister that she had some bad news.

"We only take one person from each vocation in our group, Reverend," She said. "And we already have a minister. As a matter of fact, every vocation in this community is represented in our group right now, with the exception of a hog caller. She embarrassingly asked the next question, "Would you mind being a hog caller among us?"

"Well," said the pastor, "where I come from I'm considered

a shepherd, but I suppose you know your people better than I do."[2]

You have a higher profession than a hog caller. Whether you lead a church congregation, an organization, or a business, you are a shepherd. You are called to care for those who depend on you—your sheep. Are you up to the task on your own? Or do you need some help?

Of course we all need help. And that is the great thing about the 23rd psalm: Shepherds who care for others have someone who cares for them. They all come under the provision and the protection of the Great Shepherd. Every promise or truth in Ps. 23 has your name on it!

Let's look at a few.

1. He cares about you. "The LORD is my shepherd" (v. 1, NKJV). His care is personalized. He knows you better than you know yourself. And He provides for you in ways that you will never imagine.

2. He is as concerned with your rest as He is with your responsibilities. "He makes me to lie down in green pastures" (v. 2, NKJV). Your Shepherd knows when you're too tired to go on. So He often brings circumstances into your life that will demand rest.

3. He puts His name on the line for you. "He leads me in the path of righteousness for His name's sake" (v. 3, NKJV). He paid too high a price to leave you to the wolves of hell. He fights for you with the same passion as when He died for you.

4. He provides for you. "Your rod and Your staff, they

comfort me" (v. 4, NKJV). Nothing in life or death is greater than His power and provision. You will never have to be afraid.

5. He affirms you. "You prepare a table before me in the presence of my enemies" (v. 5, NKJV). Everyone else may put you down, but He will lift you up. He's proud of you.

6. He has great plans for you. "I will dwell in the house of the LORD forever" (v. 6, NKJV). At the end of your road there is a bright beginning. Your responsibilities are temporary. His relief is eternal.

You can lead because you are being led at the same time. You can affirm others because you are being affirmed all the while.

PSALM 37

¹Do not fret because of evil men
    or be envious of those who do wrong;
²for like the grass they will soon wither,
    like green plants they will soon die away.
³Trust in the LORD and do good;
    dwell in the land and enjoy safe pasture.
⁴Delight yourself in the LORD
    and he will give you the desires of your heart.
⁵Commit your way to the LORD;
    trust in him and he will do this:
⁶He will make your righteousness shine like the dawn,
    the justice of your cause like the noonday sun.

SIX
LIFE ISN'T FAIR

So you keep honest books and don't cheat—not even a little—on your taxes. You pay good wages to your employees or staff rather than take large bonuses for yourself. You care for your assistants and listen to their advice. You place an emphasis on personal integrity.

So why are you struggling to make ends meet, while your competitor across town (whom you know to be taking ethical and, perhaps, legal shortcuts) is raking in the dough?

Is that fair? In a word: no. In two words: *That's life!*

NOTHING'S DIFFERENT

Nothing has really changed since David's day. The godless ("evil") still get blue ribbons and green bank accounts, while the godly often come in third and have "gone" accounts. So how does David address this ageless inequity? He addresses it with ageless truth! "Do not fret because of evil men" (Ps. 37:1). In other words, *Don't worry about it!*

That's it? Why didn't he call for an investigation? Why didn't he form a subcommittee to look into the injustice of evil winning over righteousness? After all, life is supposed to be played on an even field, right?

EVERYTHING WILL CHANGE

Could it be that David was given an age-old secret about life—that this world is not the end-all? That there are bottom-line results we cannot see with earthly eyes? That as C. S. Lewis would say, this is not real life. This world is merely a *shadowland?* Absolutely! David knew that the world *as we know it* isn't the world *as we shall know it.* Dr. Billy Graham said it for every follower of Christ: "I've read the last page of the Bible, and we win!"

IN THE MEANTIME

David encourages you not to get all worked up about those who prosper by doing wrong. You know that they are in every corner of life:

- A sales director pads an expense account and pockets several hundred dollars more each month.

- An author has a best-seller, even though she plagiarized a portion of her latest book.

- A pastor across town has a booming ministry, but it is known that he is having an extramarital affair.

There are many incidents where the evil are winning—for now. Psalm 37 tells us that their end won't justify their means: "For like the grass they will soon wither, like green plants they will soon die away" (v. 1). This life is but a preface to the real life—eternal life—that is to come. All the chapters haven't been written. In the last, righteousness wins and evil loses! John the Revelator got a heavenly glimpse: "And I saw the dead, small and great, stand before God; and the books were opened: and another book was opened, which is the book of life: and the dead were judged out of those things which were written in the books, according to their works" (Rev. 20:12, KJV).

WINNING PRINCIPLES

The psalmist suggests three principles for facing this temporary inequality and injustice in the corporate world or in the religious world:

1. Focus on Christ and the Kingdom. "Trust in the LORD and do good" (Ps. 37:3). The writer to the Hebrews said it another way: "Keep your eyes on Jesus, who both began and finished this race we're in. Study how he did it. Because he never lost sight of where he was headed—that exhilarating finish in and with God—he could put up with anything along the way: cross, shame, whatever. And now he's there, in the place of honor, right alongside God" (Heb. 12:2, TM).

When you are doing the good of the Kingdom, you won't have as much time to worry about what evil people are doing. Focus first on God, and then on godly goals, and *don't worry about it.*

2. Learn to be a God-pleaser. "Delight yourself in the LORD" (Ps. 37:4).

Face it, no matter how much effort you give, you won't be able to please everyone. And the longer you lead, the more you will wonder if you're able to please *anyone.* As you've already discovered, leadership is lonely. If those who work with you or for you had your gifts and your responsibilities, they'd be where you are! But since they're not at the top, they have a better angle to take potshots at you.

Understand that you don't have to please everyone. You only have to please one—God. If He is your delight, and your heart is in line with His desires, He will bless *yours*. "He will give you the desires of your heart," no matter what others may seem to accomplish.

3. Let your faith motivate your works. "Commit your way to the LORD ... and he will do this" (v. 5). The apostle James looked to the history books for a prime example: "Was not our ancestor Abraham considered righteous for what he did when he offered his son Isaac on the altar? You see that his faith and his actions were working together, and his faith was made complete by what he did" (2:21-22).

The "evil accomplishers" around you have only themselves. You have God! They may win a few skirmishes, but you serve One who won the war. You may lose once in a while, but that doesn't make you a loser. You're on the side of the Great Finisher. Philippians 1:6 says, "I am sure that God, who began the good work within you, will continue his work until it is finally finished on that day when Christ Jesus comes back again" (NLT). The world around you may make temporary gains, but every gain is a loss compared to your riches at the finish line.

PSALM 46

⁷The LORD Almighty is with us;
    the God of Jacob is our fortress.

Selah

⁸Come and see the works of the LORD,
    the desolations he has brought on the earth.
⁹He makes wars cease to the ends of the earth;
    he breaks the bow and shatters the spear,
    he burns the shields with fire.
¹⁰"Be still, and know that I am God;
    I will be exalted among the nations,
    I will be exalted in the earth."
¹¹The LORD Almighty is with us;
    the God of Jacob is our fortress.

Selah

SEVEN
QUIET!

As a leader, you're most likely in the "go" mode—leading the charge, blazing new trails, first one in, last one out. You're sure you can't stand still, because if you do, your competitor will pass you like a coyote with a rabbit one block ahead of him.

So when you hear someone telling you to stand still, you may have trouble processing it. Yet that is just what God is telling you to do in Ps. 46.

"Be still, and know that I am God" (v. 10). In other words: Quiet!

The Message paraphrase of the Bible says it this way: "Step out of the traffic! Take a long, loving look at me, your High God, above politics, above everything."

Do you remember that when your children were small, they seemed to have endless energy? They were in constant motion. You would often plead, "Can't you be still for a minute!" Do you hear God saying the same thing in this psalm? "Can't you be still for a minute?" Slow down, and step out of the traffic.

Actually, being still goes beyond tapping the breaks to slow down to the posted speed limit. It suggests coming *to a complete stop.*

Stop. Completely.

"But if I do," you say, "others will pass me by. You don't understand the nature of my business. It is changing so quickly, I have to keep running just to keep up."

God does understand your situation. He's the ultimate businessman. Among other things, He excels in agriculture and real estate. The Bible says He owns all the cattle on the thousand hills (see Ps. 50:10). He also excels in time management. He can create a planet and then landscape it in six days. He knows how fast your life is lived. He's the One who put the spin on the planets in orbit.

But He also put the sparkle in the brook. He is the Wonderful Counselor. From time to time He invites you stop what you are doing and sit quietly with Him beside the still waters. Go ahead. Step out of the traffic and take some quiet time. Listen to the still, small voice. Contemplate who God is and what He is doing in your life right now.

1. **Think about His powerful presence.** "The LORD Almighty is with us" (v. 7). There may be a hundred enemies of your plans who are conspiring against you. Stop. Think. The Lord is with you. Those who are against you are not stronger than the One who is with you. Let the power of His presence fill your thoughts. Rest your mind in the assurance that the Lord Almighty has chosen to walk with you. That's a pretty big stick!

2. **Look at His wonderful creation.** "Come and see the works of the LORD" (v. 8). Stop. Open the window. Look around you. By faith you belong to the God who created every beautiful thing that graces your eyes. Remember, He made *everything* from *nothing*. Think about it. He still can! He can take your

brokenness and make you whole. He can take your wasted efforts and make them worthwhile. He still creates everything from nothing.

3. Feel His inner peace. "He makes wars cease to the ends of the earth" (v. 9). Stop. Listen to His words to your heart. "Don't be afraid." "I am in control." "My word is the last word in all of this." Wars and conflicts have filled the pages of time. But you don't have to be at war in your heart. Feel His forgiveness. Feel His reconciliation. Feel His prompting. Relax in His promises. One day war will come to an eternal end—and you'll be there to witness the peace treaty.

4. Watch for His miraculous intervention. "Be still, and know that I am God" (v. 10). Stop. Think about the ways He is working in your life. Some projects are tenuous. But other projects are coming together. That coworker who seemed so unfriendly the other day has a smile today. That promotion or appointment that seemed so far in the horizon now seems to be drawing closer. He is at work. He does not rest. He doesn't take a time-out. He is working all things for your good—right now (Rom. 8:28).

5. Rest in His unfailing protection. "Be still, and know that I am God" (Ps. 46:11). There are many who claim to be in control of things, but they aren't. God is in control. He is your Big Brother. No, not the One who is *watching you* with doubt. He's the One who is *watching over you* with care. No one will approach you in any threatening way that has not first met His authority and judgment. Stop. Rest. God is taking care of you.

Get out of the traffic jam. Stay off the horn. Cease struggling. God doesn't worry because a process is taking too much time, so why should you? God isn't intimidated by decisions that have to be made *now*, so why should you be intimidated? His wristwatch or PDA alarm doesn't sound to tell Him it's time for the next meeting. He's always on time. Time is a tool that He uses for accomplishing His purpose through you!

Did you hear that? Time is a tool. Not a tyrant, but a tool.

God is giving you an invitation. He is inviting you to walk instead of run: to slow down long enough to have a friendly talk with a coworker; to pray with a customer; to leave your work behind for a couple of weeks and go on a short-term missions trip; to manage your hours so that you will have enough left over for family or friends; to listen for sounds you've never heard; to look at things you've never seen; to experience the life you've never lived.

PSALM 51 (NKJV)

1 Have mercy upon me, O God,

according to Your lovingkindness;

according to the multitude of Your tender mercies,

blot out my transgressions.

2 Wash me thoroughly from my iniquity,

and cleanse me from my sin.

3 For I acknowledge my transgressions,

And my sin is always before me.

4 Against You, You only, have I sinned,

and done this evil in Your sight—

that You may be found just when You speak,

and blameless when You judge.

5 Behold, I was brought forth in iniquity,

and in sin my mother conceived me.

6 Behold, You desire truth in the inward parts,

and in the hidden part You will make me to know wisdom.

7 Purge me with hyssop, and I shall be clean;

wash me, and I shall be whiter than snow.

8 Make me hear joy and gladness,

that the bones You have broken may rejoice.

9 Hide Your face from my sins,

and blot out all my iniquities.

10 Create in me a clean heart, O God,

and renew a steadfast spirit within me.

11 Do not cast me away from Your presence,

and do not take Your Holy Spirit from me.

12 Restore to me the joy of Your salvation,

and uphold me by Your generous Spirit.

13 Then I will teach transgressors Your ways,

and sinners shall be converted to You.

EIGHT
TRUE CONFESSIONS

Sometimes a leader crashes and burns. King David did.

Of all his writings, Ps. 51 had to be the most personal and likely the hardest to write. He had been caught in adultery. And he had covered up his affair by murdering the husband of the woman he slept with. He thought he had gotten away with it. Then Nathan, a prophet who answered only to God, came to him with a chilling story.

"There is a man, your highness," said Nathan, "who was but a poor farmer. He had very little of the world's goods, but what he had, he valued greatly. He only had one lamb on his whole farm, but he treasured it as if it were a child. He fed it from his own table and put it tenderly in the pen each night.

"His neighbor, on the other hand, was filthy rich. He had more sheep than he could count, and he could buy flocks of sheep at any time. One night he was hungry for lamb chops. Instead of taking an animal from his own flock, he had his servants go after the beloved lamb of his poor neighbor. That lamb was slaughtered and roasted for dinner."

The king probably jumped up from his throne and angrily pointed to the prophet. "Who is that selfish, ungrateful man? Bring him to me so he can be punished!"

Nathan, unafraid of anyone but God, looked directly at the king, pointed his finger toward the king, and said, "You are that man" (see 2 Sam. 12).

David could have had Nathan thrown out of his castle or thrown into prison. He could have spoken the word and the prophet would have been killed. How dare he accuse the king of all Israel!

But David was not so far gone that he could not feel his guilt. Nor was he so far gone that he could not seek forgiveness. Yes, he had sinned greatly. He slept with the man's beloved wife. And then, when the woman announced she was pregnant by him, King David covered his tracks by arranging the soldier-husband's death on the battlefield.

Now he was faced with his greatest challenge—greater than facing a lion or the giant Goliath. He faced a fearless prophet of God who knew his guilt. In God's eyes, the king had tumbled from the throne. David knew it. He had crashed and burned. "Against You, You only, have I sinned, and done this evil in Your sight" (Ps. 51:4, NKJV).

It would have been embarrassing for David to write about the incident were it not for one thing: When he thoroughly repented, God thoroughly forgave him! Psalm 51 is filled with both horror and hope. Leaders may fall into sin and be disgraced, but God can lift them up by His grace! Henry Ford once said, "Failure is only the opportunity to begin again more intelligently." David learned by his loss.

Most likely, you haven't killed someone to cover up a

crime. But you have sinned. We all have. Romans 3:23 says, "For all have sinned and fall short of the glory of God"; maybe not by committing adultery, but by lying or cheating or stealing or gossip or hatred in your heart or envy or disrespect.

Need we go on?

The attitudes and actions that keep you from achieving your goals may be hidden deep within your heart. But God knows your heart. He wants to free you, forgive you, untie you from your past and send you on your way. How do you respond to the inner searching of the Holy Spirit—or the valid accusations of others?

Let's look at how David responded.

1. He didn't make excuses for his behavior. He did not call his actions mistakes. You may try to deflect guilt by saying, "Everybody makes mistakes." Two plus two equals five is a mistake. But breaking God's law on purpose isn't a mistake; it's a sin. David confessed it: "I acknowledge my transgressions, and my sin is always before me" (Ps. 51:3, NKJV).

If you've stumbled or fallen, begin your road to recovery by calling your wrong actions what they are—sin. Jesus didn't die to forgive mistakes; He died to forgive sin. "He used his servant body to carry our sins to the Cross so we could be rid of sin, free to live the right way. His wounds became your healing" (1 Pet. 2:24, TM).

2. He recognized what was missing. Following his affair, David continued business as usual. Decrees were given. Ceremonies were attended. But there was a crushing ache in his heart that nothing on earth could heal: "Make me hear joy and gladness, that the bones You have broken may rejoice" (Ps. 51:8, NKJV). Business as usual is shallow and uncomfortable when there is hidden sin in your heart. Take care of the problem first and then get on with your work. Notice what the great Old Testament leader did next.

3. He asked God for forgiveness. At first he faced the prophet of God. Now in his spirit, he comes face-to-face with God himself. Notice that he doesn't boast about his crown or his kingdom; he simply pleads for mercy from the Judge of everyone's sin: "Hide Your face from my sins, and blot out all my iniquities" (v. 9, NKJV).

You won't get any free passes from sin in this life. Get Out of Jail Free cards aren't available as they are in a Monopoly game. Someone has to pay at the door. Of course there is great fallout when someone crashes and burns, but the greatest impact is personal.

Here's the good news: The spiritual debt incurred by your sin has already been paid! Jesus signed your pardon with His own blood. First John 1:7, "If we are living in the light of God's presence, just as Christ is, then we have fellowship with each other, and the blood of Jesus, his Son, cleanses us from every sin," hyperlinks beautifully to verse 9 (NLT), "If we confess our sins to him, he is faithful and just to forgive us and to cleanse us from every wrong" (NLT).

You have the same mercy David pleaded for. "Wash me, and I shall be whiter than snow" (Ps. 51:7, NKJV). This soul whitener is yours for the asking. You don't have to wear your past like a frown. You can start again—with a fresh smile. It won't happen because you made excuses. It will happen because you made a true confession.

4. He recognized his human frailty. For David, forgiveness was just the start. He realized that left to his humanity, he would only repeat his actions. So David asked for God's help: "Create in me a clean heart, O God, and renew a steadfast spirit within me" (v. 10). His new start needed a new heart. The original language suggests that this new heart isn't a remanufactured unit. It's brand-new!

He needed an inner strength—a steadfast spirit. This same steadfast spirit is available to you. Once you have been forgiven, you can be strengthened. You can surrender to the wisdom and power of the Holy Spirit. David realized he had to step off the throne of his life and let a new King take charge.

Have you relinquished control of the throne of your heart? The cycle of sin and spiritual failure can be broken. Cry out to God for His mercy. And then thank Him for His forgiveness.

PSALM 61

¹Hear my cry, O God;
    listen to my prayer.
²From the ends of the earth I call to you,
    I call as my heart grows faint;
    lead me to the rock that is higher than I.
³For you have been my refuge,
    a strong tower against the foe.
⁴I long to dwell in your tent forever
    and take refuge in the shelter of your wings.

Selah

⁵For you have heard my vows, O God;
    you have given me the heritage of those who
    fear your name.
⁶Increase the days of the king's life,
    his years for many generations.
⁷May he be enthroned in God's presence forever;
    appoint your love and faithfulness to protect
    him.
⁸Then will I ever sing praise to your name
    and fulfill my vows day after day.

NINE
A BIGGER ROCK

Prayer is one of the most important activities in the life of a leader. Prayer isn't some elaborate ceremony that takes decades of practice and a roomful of bishops to accomplish. Prayer is simply talking and listening to God. Friend to friend. Leader to supervisor. Relax, you won't surprise God with any revelation. There isn't any news alert in heaven. He knows everything you're going to say, even before you say it. And you can tell Him anything! Nothing in your life is so great that it is beyond His power. And nothing is so small that it is beyond His attention.

WHY NOT SEEK GOD'S HELP

As a leader, you are faced with numerous decisions, actions, and responsibilities every day. There could only be two reasons why you wouldn't seek God's help: One, you don't believe He can help you. Or, two, you believe you can handle everything by yourself *(thank you very much!)*.

Let's address the second reason first. David, king of Israel and a mighty warrior, had every reason to believe in himself. He had defeated a giant who was terrorizing the Israelite army. He had survived countless assassination attempts by Israel's first king, Saul. And he was much-loved by the people he led. Why did he need help? He knew he didn't have what it would take to do what needed to be done.

The past had passed. There were new challenges. Each year, month, or day brought new opportunities—and new responsibilities. He knew he couldn't rest on his laurels. The people he was leading now weren't present at the giant killing. They didn't need a legend; they needed a leader who could guide them through their current events. Consequently, David needed a new strength, new ideas, and a fresh sense of God's presence. "From the ends of the earth I call to you, I call as my heart grows faint; lead me to the rock that is higher than I" (Ps. 61:2). David didn't need a bigger kingdom to reign over; he needed a bigger rock to stand upon.

A GREATER POWER

Who was higher than the great King David? God himself, of course. David knew his limitations—and he knew there was no limitation to what God could do. He knew he could stand taller on his knees than on his throne. There was a higher place —a place of prayer.

A prayer that has circulated via the Internet says, "So far today, God, I've done all right. I haven't gossiped, haven't lost my temper, haven't been greedy, grumpy, nasty, selfish, or overindulgent. I'm really glad about that. But in a few minutes, God, I'm going to get out of bed and from then on I'm probably going to need a lot more help."

THE GOD VACUUM

There are some who don't ask for God's help because they don't believe He can give it. There is a God vacuum in their life and ministry; a vacuum that will eventually be exposed. It happened to Christ's disciples. Jesus heard about the execution of John the Baptist and went into seclusion for a time of prayer. He knew the power that His Heavenly Father had to bring about a victory over the threatening situation and bring calm to His soul during the process.

As usual, a crowd of people followed Him. And as usual, He began to teach them about the Kingdom. It was dinnertime and there weren't any fast-food restaurants nearby. The disciples were afraid that their organizational and marketing skills would be criticized, and they forgot about the miracles they had previously witnessed:

As evening approached, the disciples came to him and said, "This is a remote place, and it's already getting late. Send the crowds away, so they can go to the villages and buy themselves some food." Jesus replied, "They do not need to go away. You give them something to eat." "We have here only five loaves of bread and two fish," they answered. "Bring them here to me," he said. And he directed the people to sit down on the grass. Taking the five loaves and the two fish and looking up to heaven, he gave thanks and broke the loaves. Then he gave them to the disciples, and the disciples gave them to the people. They all ate and were satisfied, and the disciples picked up twelve basketfuls of broken pieces that were left over. The number of those who ate was about five thousand men, besides women and children (*Matt. 14:15-21*).

"We're out of food," the disciples whined. "Can God help us?" The answer was in the "twelve basketfuls" that were left over. When everything is running well, when goals are being met, employees are working hard, and your stock value is rising, you think that you have the world on a string. Who needs God?

But when stocks go south, when employees strike, when revenues fall short for two quarters in a row, who do you turn to? To paraphrase a military saying, "There are no atheists in the annual review meetings." If God isn't able to supply in the face of want or confusion, then there is no hope!

GOD IS ABLE

Fortunately, God is able, and He is concerned with all that concerns you. He will hear you when you speak to Him. Just believe in Him and commit yourself to Him. Be assured, He will do what He says He will do.

As a leader, prayer is one of your greatest responsibilities. Those who follow you are counting on you to seek God and His ways. They need you to pray for them. In fact, David reveals the value of prayer in Ps. 61.

Notice six things prayer is to the leader:

1. Prayer is the cry of a weary heart. "I call as my heart grows faint" (v. 2). Even when you've reached the end of your leadership rope, there's hope. As David's heart grew faint (during the crisis), he poured out his concern to his Heavenly Father. You're not without a solution as long as you can pray.

2. Prayer is the calm of a fearful heart. "You have been my refuge" (v. 3). Every leader looks for experience when a résumé is presented. David prayed because he knew that God had been in the answering business forever! Your road isn't new to God. And leaders before you have experienced similar situations. Those same leaders have trusted your same God.

3. Prayer is the hope of a longing heart. "I long to dwell in your tent forever" (v. 4). When you pray for your present situation, there's always a positive result in view. Prayer takes you into the present presence of an all-sufficient God. And the very act of faith-believing prayer gives you the inner assurance that all things will work together for good.

4. Prayer is the praise of a grateful heart. "You have heard my vows" (v. 5). If God couldn't multiply loaves and fishes, there would be no need to pray. The disciples made an important discovery about God—and dinner. A prayer of thanksgiving is a confession that God's eternal supply will meet your present circumstance.

5. Prayer is the trust of a faithful heart. "Appoint your love and faithfulness" (v. 7). The very character of God is the assurance of answered prayer. He loves you with an endless love. And He cares for you with an endless commitment to your need.

6. Prayer is the song of a loving heart. "I will ever

sing praise to your name and fulfill my vows" (v. 8). Just as married couples renew their marriage vows as a witness to their long-term relationship, prayer is a renewal of spiritual vows, and a witness to your relationship with God. You have given yourself to God. You are known by His name. And the result of that relationship is pure joy!

The great leader of the Early Church, the apostle Paul, comforted those who followed his leadership. He let them know he held them up in prayer: "In all my prayers for all of you, I always pray with joy because of your partnership in the gospel from the first day until now, being confident of this, that he who began a good work in you will carry it on to completion until the day of Christ Jesus" (Phil. 1:4-6).

That prayer had to be of great comfort to those embattled first-century Christians who were going through the fires of opposition. Knowing their leader was praying for them would keep them going, even in the face of great difficulty.

And knowing that God was listening to that leader's prayers was an even greater incentive to be his representative.

PSALM 82

[1]God presides in the great assembly;
    he gives judgment among the "gods":
[2]"How long will you defend the unjust
    and show partiality to the wicked?

                      Selah

[3]Defend the cause of the weak and fatherless;
    maintain the rights of the poor and oppressed.
[4]Rescue the weak and needy;
    deliver them from the hand of the wicked.
[5]They know nothing, they understand nothing.
    They walk about in darkness;
    all the foundations of the earth are shaken.
[6]I said, 'You are "gods";
    you are all sons of the Most High.'
[7]But you will die like mere men;
    you will fall like every other ruler."
[8]Rise up, O God, judge the earth,
    for all the nations are your inheritance.

TEN
JUDGING JUDGES

No one likes to be called on the carpet. Receiving the call or e-mail that we are to appear before our boss, or worse yet our boss's boss, can ruin a good day. Immediately we think, "What have I done now?" Or maybe the problem is we *know* what we've done!

Getting a summons to appear in court can be unnerving as well. When we go before a judge in a court of law, we will either be afraid that justice won't be done or that it will. Either way, if we are guilty, we know there will be consequences.

Imagine being called in front of the Judge of all judges—the Chief Justice of the Supreme Court of Heaven. That is what this psalm is about. Asaph, a leader of King David's choir, starts off Ps. 82 by saying God has called earthly judges into His courtroom (v. 1). And it wasn't going to be a social gathering—unless you consider it a going-away party.

In the times of Asaph and David, judges had great powers. They made judgments concerning legal, moral, and religious matters. Asaph, an inspired author who assisted David in the writing of the Psalms, outlines what the judges were supposed to do: "You're here to defend the defenseless, to make sure that underdogs get a fair break; your job is to stand up for the powerless, and prosecute all those who exploit them" (vv. 3-4, TM).

The judges summoned to the great assembly had looked the other way when a crime was committed. Murderers were pardoned. Robbers were given handshakes instead of handcuffs. Wickedness ruled over the good. Oppression was winning over the weak. And now it was time for accountability.

In one sense, as a leader you are as responsible as the judges of Asaph's day. You have been given responsibility for those whom you lead. How does that play out in the office, church, or home? Notice three important leadership tasks in Ps. 82:

1. Defend the defenseless. "Defend the cause of the weak" (v. 3a). The scope of your leadership is very broad. It not only involves those under your immediate supervision but also reaches those who surround them. Leadership without a driving passion to right the wrong is not Christlike leadership. You serve One who could not settle for the status quo—One whose very life was offered in defense of the defenseless.

That sacrifice may be exemplified in other ways in your life. Your cause may be the attempt to restore values in the organizational workplace. You may be concerned with alleviating the financial, emotional, or physical abuse of a worker or staff member. You may take a stand between a staff member and his or her accusers. Whatever the situation may be, where someone is weak, the leader is there to shore them up—in a way that would honor Christ and bring a sense of value to that person.

2. Assist the needy. "Maintain the rights of the poor and oppressed" (v. 3b). Jesus set the bar. Assisting those in need was not only a primary concern but also a primary requirement for His followers:

> "For I was hungry and you gave me something to eat, I was thirsty and you gave me something to drink, I was a stranger and you invited me in, I needed clothes and you clothed me, I was sick and you looked after me, I was in prison and you came to visit me." Then the righteous will answer him, "Lord, when did we see you hungry and feed you, or thirsty and give you something to drink? When did we see you a stranger and invite you in, or needing clothes and clothe you? When did we see you sick or in prison and go to visit you?" The King will reply, "I tell you the truth, whatever you did for one of the least of these brothers of mine, you did for me" *(Matt. 25:35-40).*

3. Empower the powerless. "Rescue the weak and needy" (Ps. 82:4). As a leader you are a first responder. You have the resources and opportunity to extricate someone from the debris. Some are trapped by the incidents of their past. Others have been crushed by their addictions. And others are mired in negative thinking. You have an opportunity to free them—to cause them to look beyond their present situation to a bright future and a new beginning. It won't take long to discern those under your supervision who are struggling with more than a flow chart or a parking space. The Holy Spirit will show you those who need a hand of encouragement. Those who need tough love to overcome tough situations. "Stoop down and reach out to those who are oppressed. Share their burdens, and so complete Christ's law" (Gal. 6:2, TM).

As a leader, you are responsible for the efforts of the led. You are also responsible to fill in the gaps of their life with knowledge, compassion, correction, and affirmation. This is not for the weak of heart or the weak of faith. Being responsible for others is a daunting challenge. That is why great leaders are so hard to find.

The leadership challenge isn't the shortage of people who would like to have power and privilege. It is the difficulty in finding those who are willing to carry others on their shoulders, people who will be willing to get down from the judge's bench and lift the fallen—men and women who won't be afraid to show support for the weak and to chase off those who prey on the powerless.

PSALM 105

¹Give thanks to the LORD, call on his name;
>   make known among the nations what he has
>   done.
²Sing to him, sing praise to him;
>   tell of all his wonderful acts.
³Glory in his holy name;
>   let the hearts of those who seek the LORD
>   rejoice.
⁴Look to the LORD and his strength;
>   seek his face always.
⁵Remember the wonders he has done,
>   his miracles, and the judgments he pronounced.

ELEVEN
JOB DESCRIPTION

You've probably written a job description. Hopefully you haven't been in the position of the pastor whose church board asked him to come up with his own job description. He wrote an in-depth description of what he felt were the things a pastor ought to be doing for that church. At the next board meeting the pastor was told that his job description had been enthusiastically accepted. The board chairman then announced, "Now all we have to do is to find someone who fits this description!"

DUTIES

Have you ever thought of what a leader's job description would look like? What does God expect of us anyway? If you were applying for a "follower of Jesus" leadership position, what would your duties be?

Psalm 105 gives us some of those duties.

1. Give thanks to the Lord. Christians are to be thankful people. God does great things for His followers—even in ways unseen. And as parents would expect their children to say "Thank you" for earthly gifts, your Heavenly Father asks you to be grateful for heavenly gifts. If you remember it is one of your job duties, something that will be evaluated at your final review, you would be careful to say thank You when the Lord gives to you.

2. Call on His name. God gave a word of advice to the leader-prophet Jeremiah: "Call to Me, and I will answer you, and show you great and mighty things, which you do not know" (Jer. 33:3, NKJV). There shouldn't be any Lone Rangers in God's army. There are only soldiers who wait for commands and instructions from their Commanding Officer. The inference in God's instructions to Jeremiah is the same to every Christian: You'll know how to carry out your earthly duties once you seek heavenly advice!

3. Make known what He has done. Christian leadership is the marketing arm of Christianity. You are not to leave it up to some hired agency to let others know how great God is. That's your job! Psalm 105:1 suggests that whether in plans, words, actions, or attitudes, your faith—and God's faithfulness—should be "known among the nations."

4. Sing praises to Him. Most of us wouldn't make the last round of an "American Idol" competition. And your voice may have the quality of a malfunctioning foghorn. Singing may not be in your list of job requirements. But singing praise is! You've heard someone talk about singing the praises of another person. A Christian's job duties include singing the praises of Jesus. The poet Katherine Hankey reflected on it in a gospel song: "I love to tell the story / Of unseen things above, / Of Jesus and His glory, / Of Jesus and His love."

5. Rejoice. There it is in black and white! "Let the hearts of those who seek the LORD rejoice" (v. 3). Part of your job as a Christian is to be happy! And why not? You are a follower of the

King of the universe. You are on the winning team. You don't have a cemetery ending; you have a heavenly ending. When you finish your work *here,* you'll move to a new home somewhere out *there.*

6. Seek the Lord. Verse 4 says to "Look to the LORD." No, God isn't playing hide and seek with you. The psalmist's writing suggests that you need to keep your eyes on God and follow where He leads. Look to Him as your first source of advice and your first line of defense.

7. Remember what He has done. Verse 5 says, "Remember the wonders he has done." One of your duties as a Christian is to inventory the great things God has done in your life and in the lives of others. Read the books of the Old and New Testament. Read biographies of Christian leaders who have gone before you. Catalog God's goodness in their lives. Think of the greatness of God often. Fall asleep thinking of His faithfulness to faithless Israel or wake up rejoicing with the Early Church over its survival from enemy fire.

BENEFITS

You probably wouldn't take a job without knowing its salary and benefits. Neither would those who work for you—or with you. In an age when we almost need insurance to cover our insurance coverage, knowing both the salary and the benefits is imperative.

When it comes to salary in the Corporation of the Kingdom, there is often inequity—especially in comparison to the secular corporate world. But the benefits are incomparable! God has a complete benefits package for those who choose to follow Him. It can be seen in Ps. 103: "Bless the LORD, O my soul, and forget not all His benefits: who forgives all your iniquities, who heals all your diseases, who redeems your life from destruction, who crowns you with lovingkindness and tender mercies, who satisfies your mouth with good things, so that your youth is renewed like the eagle's" (vv. 2-5, NKJV).

Notice at least six parts to this comprehensive plan:

1. Workers compensation. One of your benefits covers your injury while on the job. What leader hasn't suffered the hurts of criticism? What leader hasn't experienced the pain of failure? And what leader hasn't experienced the crippling weight of responsibility? God knows. "For God is not unfair. He will not forget how hard you have worked for him and how you have shown your love to him by caring for other Christians, as you still do" (Heb. 6:10, NLT).

2. Health coverage. What a medical plan! Are you sick? God will take care of it. You're His employee—and one of your benefits is spiritual healing. Any and all diseases, including existing conditions, are eligible in this plan!

3. Buy-out. God put a clause in your spiritual contract that promises you a spiritual buy-out. Are you old enough to remember when you would take empty pop bottles back to the grocery store and get a nickel in return? It was called redeeming the empty. In essence, the store bought the bottle back from you. God does the same for those who follow Him. He buys your life back. It doesn't matter what shape it's in. Beaten and battered, broken and bruised—He buys you back from destruction.

4. Guaranteed bonuses. God's love is not conditional like human love. He does not say, "I will love you if you do thus and so." Those who join His company are guaranteed His love and compassion. However, the supply of His love is limitless and available to His whole creation!

5. Paid vacation. Instead of putting you out to pasture, God renews your youth like the eagle's. An eagle goes through periods of renewal where he plucks out his worn-out and damaged feathers, then waits in safety as new feathers take their place. In this way, an eagle is renewed and able to do all he could in his youth. God does the same for His followers—He replaces worn-out strength with brand-new strength so they can keep on going.

6. Life insurance. Your life, as well as your work, is temporary. It is subject to the effects of time. So God promises you an eternal compensation. Not only will your work survive your efforts, but you also will survive your work! That means eternal life in the presence of the CEO of heaven.

Being a follower of Jesus is a great opportunity!

PSALM 139

¹O Lᴏʀᴅ, you have searched me
    and you know me.
²You know when I sit and when I rise;
    you perceive my thoughts from afar.
³You discern my going out and my lying down;
    you are familiar with all my ways.
⁴Before a word is on my tongue
    you know it completely, O Lᴏʀᴅ.
⁵You hem me in—behind and before;
    you have laid your hand upon me.

TWELVE
WHO OWNS YOUR HOME?

If you've ever sold a home, you know the pressures of an open house. Great pains are taken to make sure the home will look well kept when a potential buyer arrives. Then again, if you still inhabit the home, there are some areas that are off limits: The closet that has become a catchall. Or the guestroom filled with boxes and serving as a staging area for a move to another home. You've watched nervously as the potential buyer does a walk-through, examining the kitchen, the great room, the dining room, and the bedrooms. You want to make a good impression.

Leadership is often subjected to an open house. A supervisor or an organizational board does a walk-through, measuring your performance in comparison to your job description. It was the same for King David: "O LORD, you have searched me and you know me" (Ps. 139:1). Nothing escaped the Holy Spirit's evaluation. That must have been both unsettling and comforting to the king. The One who knew him best, who created him and sustained him, reviewed his life and his work.

THE REVIEW

David's leadership was reviewed in several areas—areas that are representative in your leadership.

I. David's work ethic was reviewed. "You know when I sit and when I rise" (v. 2a). Your life is measured in minutes and hours, as well as days and weeks and years. And every minute counts. You only have a brief moment in time to accomplish your part in God's eternal purpose. Jesus recognized that in His earthly ministry. He told His disciples, "All of us must quickly carry out the tasks assigned us by the one who sent me, because there is little time left before the night falls and all work comes to an end" (John 9:4, NLT). That purpose-driven urgency is a great plus for a third millennium leader. The night is falling. What we are called to accomplish must be accomplished now!

2. David's thought life was reviewed. "You perceive my thoughts" (Ps. 139:2b). In one sense, you are what you think. Your thought life can bring you great success or great failure. It must be under control. There are things your heart must not be subjected to. There are attitudes that must not be given rental space in your mind.

3. David's actions were reviewed. "You are familiar with all my ways" (v. 3). One of the great tricks of the devil is to trade the necessary for the most convenient. Leadership goals are often missed when the leader gets sidetracked. Recreation takes over. Hobbies come first. Finances are unkempt.

4. David's speech was reviewed. "Before a word is on my tongue you know it" (v. 4). You are known by your words. Kind words will commend you. Thoughtless words will condemn you. Great leaders are tongue tamers. The apostle James warned, "It only takes a spark, remember, to set off a forest fire.

A careless or wrongly placed word out of your mouth can do that. By our speech we can ruin the world, turn harmony to chaos, throw mud on a reputation, send the whole world up in smoke and go up in smoke with it, smoke right from the pit of hell" (3:5-6, TM).

THE APPROVAL

King David passed his examination with high scores. Why? Not because of his actions but because of his allegiance. "You hem me in . . . you have laid your hand upon me" (Ps. 139:5). David recognized where his strength came from. He couldn't even get some sun on the roof of his castle without putting his life in jeopardy. He knew the failure of wandering eyes and wandering thoughts and wandering commitments. He had experienced God's recovery. There was no turning back. God was the only solution for the survival of his leadership.

David gave God his heart and that made all the difference. It still does. There is a great little booklet written by Robert Boyd Munger called *My Heart, Christ's Home*. Scarcely 2,200 words long, it tells of inviting Jesus into one's home, only to block His entrance into various rooms.

In the end, the author realizes that he needs Jesus' help in *every* room of his life. He asks Him to take over the management of his heart. The result is heartwarming. In Munger's book, Christ responds to the invitation:

His face lit up as He replied, "I'd love to! That is what I want to do. You cannot be a victorious Christian in your own strength. Let me do it through you and for you. That is the way. But," He added slowly, "I am just a guest. I have no authority to proceed, since the property is not mine."

Dropping to my knees, I said, "Lord, You have been a guest and I have been a host. From now on I am going to be the servant. You are going to be the owner and Master."[3]

Have you asked Jesus to make your heart His home? Have you given Him the keys and the deed? If so, you are following the greatest Leader of all and becoming the leader He wants you to be.

NOTES

1. J. C. Watts (public message, heard by Stan Toler when J. C. spoke at church in Oklahoma City).

2. This joke is adapted from a story widely available on the Internet. One version is found at http://www.jokesinthemail.com/religion-jokes/ hogcaller.htm (accessed August 30, 2006).

3. Robert Boyd Munger, *My Heart, Christ's Home,* booklet ed. (Downers Grove, Ill.: InterVarsity Press, 1986).

ABOUT THE AUTHORS

STAN TOLER

Stan Toler is founder of the Vibrant Group and is senior pastor of Trinity Church of the Nazarene in Oklahoma City. For several years he taught seminars for John Maxwell's INJOY Group, a Christian leadership development institute. He currently serves as executive director of the Toler Leadership Center, located on the Oklahoma City campus of Mid-America Christian University. Toler has written over 50 books, including his best-sellers *God Has Never Failed Me, but He's Sure Scared Me to Death a Few Times; The Buzzards Are Circling, but God's Not Finished with Me Yet; God's Never Late, He's Seldom Early, He's Always Right on Time;* his popular Minute Motivators series; and his latest book, *The Secret Blend.*

For additional information on seminars, to schedule speaking engagements, or to contact the author—

Stan Toler
P.O. Box 892170
Oklahoma City, OK 73189-2170
stoler1107@aol.com
www.stantoler.com

JERRY BRECHEISEN

Jerry Brecheisen (pronounced BRECK-eye-zen) is an author, humorist, speaker, and musician who currently serves as director of media for The Wesleyan Church and managing editor of *Wesleyan Life* magazine. He has authored 14 books and writes the weekly online column *Hope Above the Headlines*. Jerry and his wife, Carol, have two children and four grandchildren and reside in Fishers, Indiana.

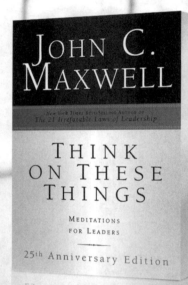
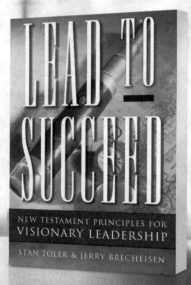

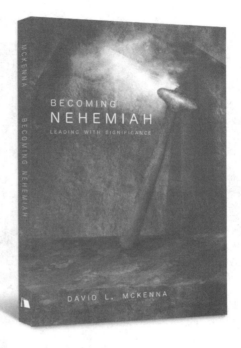